Stephon Marbury

THE STORY OF THE PHOENIX SUNS

Charles Barkley

A HISTORY OF HOOPS

THE STORY OF THE

PHOENIX SUNS

JIM WHITING

CREATIVE SPORTS

Goran Dragić

CREATIVE EDUCATION / CREATIVE PAPERBACKS

Published by Creative Education and Creative Paperbacks
P.O. Box 227, Mankato, Minnesota 56002
Creative Education and Creative Paperbacks are imprints of
The Creative Company
www.thecreativecompany.us

Design and production by Blue Design (www.bluedes.com)
Art direction by Rita Marshall

Photographs by AP Images (Associated Press), Corbis (Mark Halmas/Icon SMI),
Getty (Andrew D. Bernstein, Dylan Buell, Hank Delespinasse, James Drake,
Stephen Dunn, G. Fiume, Barry Gossage, Kelsey Grant, Andy Hayt, John Iacono,
Jed Jacobsohn, John W. McDonough, Fernando Medina, Manny Millan, NBA
Photo Library, New York Daily News Archive, Christian Petersen, Dick Raphael),
© Steve Lipofsky, Newscom (Andrew Gombert, Ting Shen/Xinhua/Photoshot),
USPresswire (David Butler II), Wikimedia Commons (Public Domain)

Library of Congress Cataloging-in-Publication Data
Names: Whiting, Jim, 1943- author.
Title: The story of the Phoenix Suns / by Jim Whiting.
Description: Mankato, Minnesota : Creative Education and Creative
    Paperbacks, [2023] | Series: Creative Sports: A History of Hoops |
    Includes index. | Audience: Ages 8-12 |
    Audience: Grades 4-6 | Summary: "Middle grade basketball fans are
    introduced to the extraordinary history of NBA's Phoenix Suns with a
    photo-laden narrative of their greatest successes and losses"-- Provided
    by publisher.
Identifiers: LCCN 2022016895 (print) | LCCN 2022016896 (ebook) | ISBN
    9781640266407 (library binding) | ISBN 9781682771969 (paperback) | ISBN
    9781640007819 (pdf)
Subjects: LCSH: Phoenix Suns (Basketball team)--Juvenile literature. |
    Basketball--United States--History--Juvenile literature.
Classification: LCC GV885.1 .W535 2023 (print) | LCC GV885.1 (ebook) |
    DDC 796.323640973--dc23
LC record available at https://lccn.loc.gov/2022016895
LC ebook record available at https://lccn.loc.gov/2022016896

Grant Hill

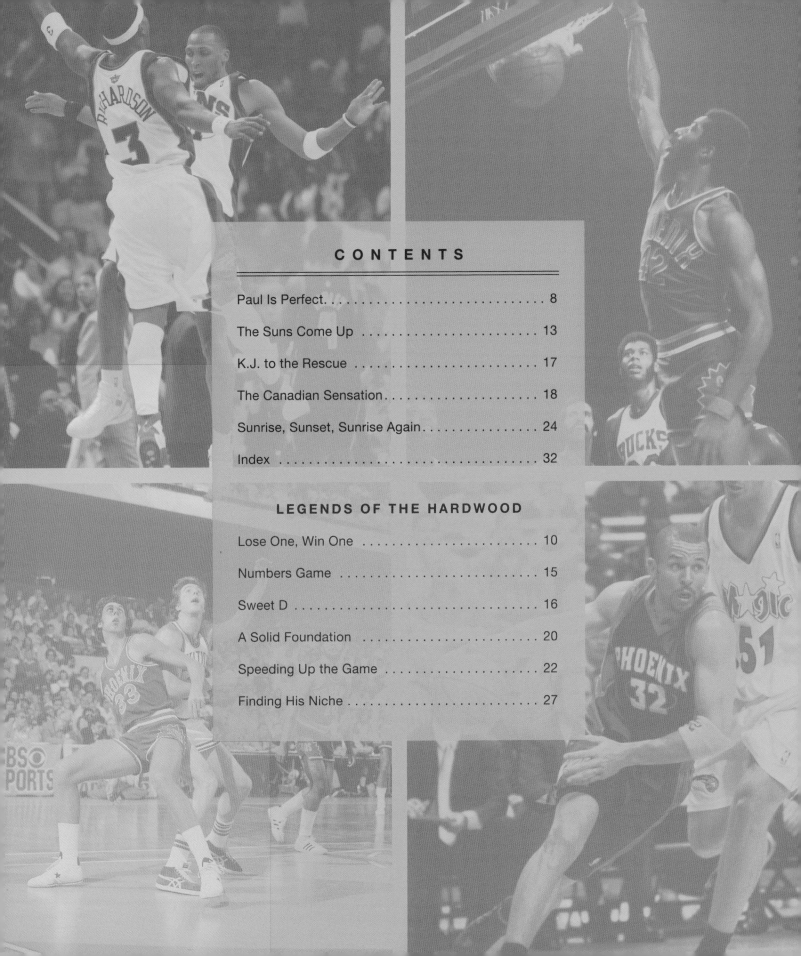

CONTENTS

LEGENDS OF THE HARDWOOD

PAUL IS PERFECT

The Phoenix Suns won 64 games in the 2021–22 National Basketball Association (NBA) season. It was the team's highest-ever win total and gave them the top overall seed in the playoffs. They faced New Orleans in the first round. The Pelicans had barely squeezed in. Many people thought Phoenix would sweep the series. They didn't. The teams split the first two games. The Suns won Game 3 by just three points. New Orleans won Game 4. After the Suns won Game 5, the Pelicans took a 10-point halftime lead in Game 6. If they held on, they would have the chance to become just the sixth 8-seed to defeat a 1-seed in NBA history.

Phoenix point guard Chris Paul hit a jump shot with just over six minutes left in the third quarter to put the Suns ahead, 70–69. The Pelicans didn't fold. They took a three-point lead into the final quarter. The lead went back and forth. Paul's two free throws with a minute left put Phoenix ahead, 110–104. Moments later, a Pelicans three-point play put them within three points of the lead. Paul hit a 12-foot jump shot with 28 seconds left. It iced the game as Phoenix won 115–109. The Suns won the series, 4 games to 2. They moved on to the next round of the playoffs.

Paul made all 14 of his field goal attempts that night. It is a feat unmatched in NBA history. "Chris did something historical tonight," said coach Monty Williams. "We needed it to win a game like this."

Chris Paul

LEGENDS OF THE HARDWOOD

Kareem Abdul-Jabbar

Connie Hawkins

LOSE ONE, WIN ONE

After their first year, the Suns and the Bucks ranked
at the bottom of the NBA standings. A coin toss would
determine which picked first in the 1969 NBA Draft.
The winner would select superstar Lew Alcindor (now
Kareem Abdul-Jabbar). A Phoenix newspaper held a
poll to see what the Suns should call. Heads, said the
fans. The coin came up tails. Fans always wondered,
"What if?" "We had a group of young guys that would
have fit perfectly with Alcindor," said Jerry Colangelo.
"We would have been in a prime position to have
a good long run if we had won that coin flip." The
Suns did better soon afterward. The NBA staged a
coin toss between them and the Seattle SuperSonics
for the rights to Connie Hawkins. The Suns won. A
Phoenix newspaper columnist said it was "the greatest
comeback in coin-flipping history."

The team's 2021–22 record was almost the mirror image of its first year in the NBA in 1968–69. The Suns had a 16–66 mark that year. It was the league's worst record that season and still remains the worst in team history.

Help was on the way. New York City prep sensation Cornelius "Connie" Hawkins had been caught up in a college point-shaving scandal in 1961, even though he was completely innocent. No college would admit him. No NBA team would draft him. He played a season in the American Basketball League, four seasons with the Harlem Globetrotters, and then two more in the American Basketball Association (ABA). "He would dominate the game," said ABA teammate and fellow All-Star Charles Williams. "Connie used to make some moves in practice and then ask for feedback. It was a pleasure watching him fly through the air."

Eventually he filed a lawsuit against the NBA. He claimed that the league had unfairly barred him. Several major media outlets had examined the "evidence" against him. The league concluded that it would lose the lawsuit. They gave him a $1.3 million settlement. His rights were awarded to the Suns.

Hawkins proved that he belonged in the NBA. He averaged nearly 24 points, 10 rebounds, and 5 assists per game in 1969–70. He was named to the All-NBA First Team. The Suns improved to 39 wins. They qualified for the playoffs, where they faced the long-established Los Angeles Lakers. Phoenix lost the first game. Hawkins had 34 points, 20 rebounds, and 7 assists to lead the Suns to a 114–101 upset in Game 2. "That was the greatest individual performance I've ever seen," said Suns coach Jerry Colangelo. Phoenix shocked the basketball world by winning the next two games as well. The Lakers surged back to take the next three games and win the series.

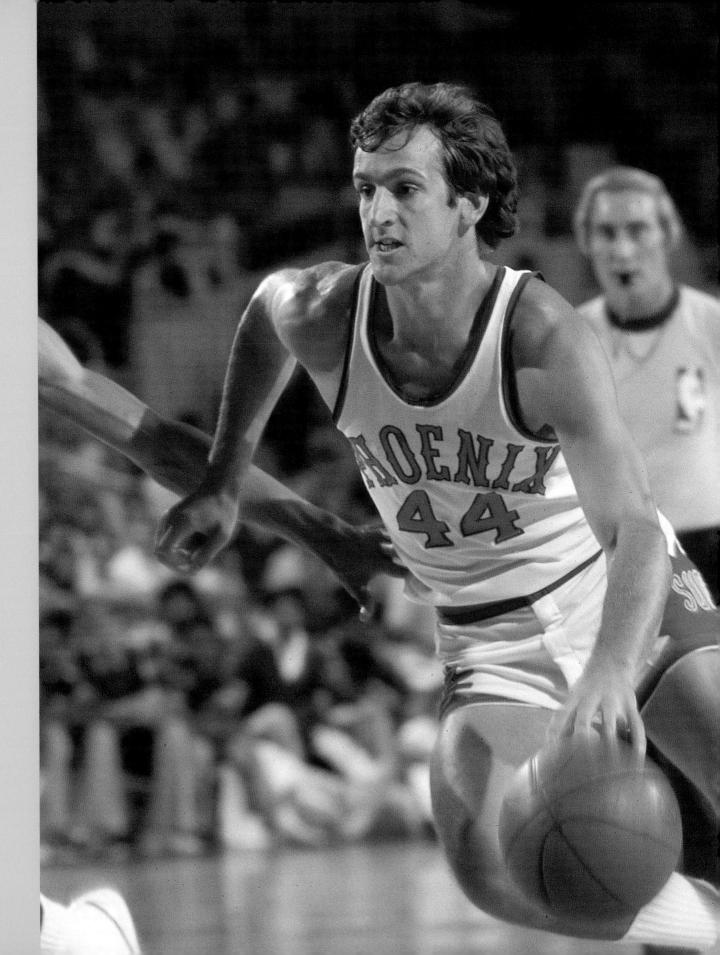

THE SUNS COME UP

Phoenix won 48 and 49 games the next two seasons. But only the top two teams in each of the league's four divisions made the playoffs. Milwaukee and Chicago finished ahead of the Suns in the Midwest Division both times. Phoenix posted losing records in the next three seasons. The playoffs were becoming a distant memory. So was Hawkins's brilliance. By then, he had a serious knee surgery. He was traded to the Lakers early in the 1973–74 season. Nearly 30 years later, Hawkins was finally enshrined in the Basketball Hall of Fame. He was the first Suns player to receive that honor.

Phoenix traded for guard Paul Westphal and power forward Gar Heard before the 1975–76 season. They drafted center Alvan Adams. He was NBA Rookie of the Year. It still took more than half the season for the team to gain traction. They finished 42–40. They caught fire in the playoffs. Phoenix beat the Seattle SuperSonics in the first round. Then they knocked off the defending NBA champion Golden State Warriors in seven games. The Suns were in the NBA Finals for the first time.

After losing the first two games of the Finals to Boston, the Suns battled back to tie the series. Game 5 went to triple overtime. In the second overtime period, Heard sank a high arching 20-foot shot as time expired that tied the game again. Phoenix fans call it "the shot heard 'round the world." That is a reference to Ralph Waldo Emerson's poem "Concord Hymn," about the Battle of Lexington

Paul Westphal

Curtis Perry in 1976 NBA Finals

in 1775 and the start of the Revolutionary War. Boston won by two points in the third overtime. "That was the most exciting basketball game I've ever seen," said broadcaster Rick Barry. "They just had one great play after another." A late Celtics surge in Game 6 gave Boston the championship.

The Suns stumbled down to 34 wins the following season. They rebounded to 49 wins in 1977–78. Small forward Walter Davis was NBA Rookie of the Year. But the Suns lost in the first round of the playoffs. Phoenix had a franchise-best 50 wins the following season. It easily advanced to the Western Conference finals against Seattle. After losing the first two games, Phoenix took the next three. They trailed by only a point with less than a minute to go in Game 6 but missed three scoring opportunities and lost. Seattle took a big lead in the decisive Game 7. The Suns closed to within two points with four seconds remaining before losing.

Phoenix had early playoff exits in the next four seasons. They had a 41–41 record in 1983–84. Just like in 1976, they caught fire in the playoffs. They faced the Lakers in the Western Conference finals. Los Angeles boasted superstars Kareem

ALVAN ADAMS
POWER FORWARD/CENTER
HEIGHT: 6-FOOT-9
SUNS SEASONS: 1975–88

LEGENDS
OF THE HARDWOOD

NUMBERS GAME

Alvan Adams was the fourth overall pick in the 1975 NBA
Draft. He was a quiet man. He didn't pump himself up or
glare at his opponents. Weighing just 220 pounds, Adams
didn't seem bulky enough to mix it up around the hoop. He
quickly proved his doubters wrong. "He didn't necessarily
look the part, but he went out and played hard every night,"
said coach John MacLeod. Adams wore number 33 in honor
of Kareem Abdul-Jabbar, who wore that number at UCLA. "I
figured he was the big guy for UCLA and I was the big guy for
our team so that was the way I wanted to go." Adams played
his entire career in Phoenix. He is the team's all-time leading
rebounder and ranks second in scoring.

PHOENIX SUNS

15

WALTER DAVIS

SMALL FORWARD/SHOOTING GUARD

HEIGHT: 6-FOOT-6

SUNS SEASONS: 1977–88

SWEET D

Walter Davis's teammate Alvan Adams called him "one of the great shooters in NBA history. I don't remember a sweeter shot." This gift was on full display on February 25, 1983 against the Seattle SuperSonics. Davis sank his first field goal attempt. And the second. And the third. And so on. At one point, Adams asked himself, "Should I go to the offensive boards [when Davis shot]? No. He's going to make it anyway." Davis eventually put down 15 shots in a row. He added four free throws. His 34 points set an NBA record for most total points scored without a miss. With less than a minute left, Davis finally missed. Even that worked out for the best. Phoenix power forward Larry Nance put the rebound into the basket while being fouled. His three-point play helped Phoenix to a 106–101 victory.

Abdul-Jabbar and Magic Johnson. The Lakers were heavy favorites. Los Angeles took a 3–1 series edge. Phoenix won Game 5. A last-second Phoenix shot fell just short in Game 6 as the Lakers escaped with a 99–97 win to close out the series.

K.J. TO THE RESCUE

The Suns dipped to 36 wins the following season. They squeaked into the playoffs. They faced the Lakers in the first round. This time it was no contest. The Lakers averaged 136 points a game and swept the series. Phoenix won just 32 games in 1985–86. They missed the playoffs for the first time in nine years.

Team officials added rookie point guard Kevin Johnson in a trade during the 1987–88 season. "K. J." was a perfect fit. "It didn't take long to know that he was special," Colangelo said. "He turned out to be better than we anticipated." He averaged more than 20 points and 12 assists a game in 1988–89. The league named him the Most Improved Player. Phoenix went from 28 wins to 55. It was one of the biggest one-year turnarounds in NBA history. Unfortunately, Phoenix faced the Lakers again in the Western Conference finals. Once again Los Angeles swept the series.

Phoenix finally turned the tables the following season. Los Angeles had the best record in the NBA. The Suns beat them in the Western Conference semifinals, 4 games to 1. But they couldn't get by Portland in the next round. Johnson said, "We just needed to get a little stronger … and find that toughness we needed."

That toughness arrived in 1992–93. The Suns traded for power forward Charles Barkley. Barkley was a ferocious rebounder and high scorer. The combination of K. J. and Barkley resulted in an NBA-best 62 wins. Barkley was named NBA Most Valuable Player (MVP). The Suns knocked off Seattle in the Western Conference finals. Before the deciding Game 7, Barkley promised 40 points and 20 rebounds. He lived up to his word with 44 points and 24 rebounds. But the Suns lost in the Finals to Michael Jordan and the Chicago Bulls, 4 games to 2. Every game was decided by 10 points or less.

Phoenix continued playing well in the next two seasons. Both times they faced the Houston Rockets in the Western Conference semifinals. Both times they took a 3 games to 2 lead. Both times the Rockets won the final two games. The Suns slid to 41 wins in 1995–96 and 40 the following season. By then Barkley was gone. Phoenix surged to 56 wins in 1997–98. The San Antonio Spurs knocked them out of the playoffs in the first round. Johnson retired.

THE CANADIAN SENSATION

The Suns continued playing at a high level for the next three years. One reason was small forward Shawn Marion. He was the team's top draft pick in 1999. But Phoenix still struggled in the playoffs. They missed the playoffs completely in 2001–02. It was the first time in 14 years without a playoff berth. Players such as power forward Amar'e Stoudamire helped the team return to the playoffs the following season. But they fell to just 29 wins in 2003–04.

Kevin Johnson

STEVE NASH
POINT GUARD
HEIGHT: 6-FOOT-3
SUNS SEASONS:
1996–98, 2004–12

A SOLID FOUNDATION

Canadian-born Steve Nash was a two-time MVP and six-time All-Star with Phoenix. He was especially noted for his selfless play. He is far more than a basketball player. Some people call him "Can-Je." That's short for "Canadian Jesus." It refers to the large number of charities he supports through his Steve Nash Foundation. The Foundation's reach is global: aiding war-torn children in Uganda, building a pediatric cardiology ward in Paraguay, organizing exhibition games in China that raised millions of dollars to help the country's children. In 2006, *Time* magazine named him one of the 100 Most Influential People in the World. He received the Order of Canada, the country's civilian honor, the following year.

The solution to the Suns' problems was Canadian-born All-Star point guard Steve Nash, who rejoined the team for the 2004–05 season. They had drafted him in 1996. He proved to be a disappointment and was traded after his second season. Nash was vastly improved since then. He was not only a great shooter but also knew how to spread the ball around.

"It was no secret as to how good Steve was before he got here," said coach Mike D'Antoni. "But once you see him operate day after day, it was a pretty awesome experience." That experience helped Phoenix surge to 62 wins. It was the best record in the league. Nash was named MVP. Phoenix made it to the Western Conference finals. But they lost to the Spurs, 4 games to 1. Nash repeated as MVP the following season. The Suns advanced to the conference finals again. This time they lost to the Dallas Mavericks, 4 games to 2.

Nash nearly won a third straight MVP title in 2006–07. Only three players had accomplished that feat. He finished second in the voting. The Suns won 61 games that season. They bowed out in the Western Conference semifinals. Massive center Shaquille O'Neal joined the team midway through the 2007–08 season. Phoenix won 55 games that season. But they lost in the first round of the playoffs. O'Neal's bulk helped on defense. But he wasn't a good fit for the Suns' fast-break offense. He moved on.

SPEEDING UP THE GAME

Many teams in the early 2000s were built around a dominating but plodding big man. Coach Mike D'Antoni had always wanted to run a fast-paced, run-and-gun style of offense. In 2004, he began a style known as "Seven seconds or less." It meant that the team wanted to put up a shot within seven seconds of gaining possession. D'Antoni moved mobile power forward Amar'e Stoudamire to center. Point guard Steve Nash would quickly bring the ball up court. He had several options: a pick-and-roll with Stoudamire, attack the basket himself, let Stoudamire put up a shot, or pass to one of three athletic wing players such as Shawn Marion for mid-to-long range jumpers. It worked. The team tied its franchise-best 62 wins. They won 54, 61, and 55 games the next three seasons. But despite several deep playoff runs, Phoenix couldn't win the title. Marion and D'Antoni were gone after 2008. Stoudamire had injury issues. "Seven seconds or less" ended. Its influence didn't. Many teams today run very similar offenses.

Amare Stoudemire

PHOENIX SUNS

SUNRISE, SUNSET, SUNRISE AGAIN

The Suns rose again in 2009–10. Phoenix easily advanced to the Western Conference finals. But the Lakers took the series, 4 games to 2. "This is as special a group as I've been involved with," Nash said after the series. "I'd love to keep [the team] together." He didn't get his wish. Several key players left. Phoenix missed the playoffs the next two seasons.

The Suns traded Nash. Without his leadership, the team slumped to just 25 wins in 2012–13. Many experts thought they would do even worse in the following season. Yet they finished 48–34. One reason for the improvement was shooting guard Eric Bledsoe. He averaged nearly 18 points a game. But Phoenix missed the playoffs by a single game. They didn't come close to the playoffs the following season.

Things got even worse in 2015–16. Bledsoe was injured early in the season. The Suns played below expectations. They won only 23 games. That was the second-worst record in franchise history. Only the team's first season, 47 years earlier, was worse. It also marked the sixth straight year in which Phoenix failed to reach the playoffs. The losing continued. The worst came in 2018–19. The Suns won only 19 games.

Phoenix improved to 34 wins in the COVID-19-shortened 2019–20 season. That set the stage for 2020–21. Sixteen-year veteran point guard Chris Paul joined the team. Shooting guard Devin Booker averaged more than 25 points a game. He

Jared Dudley

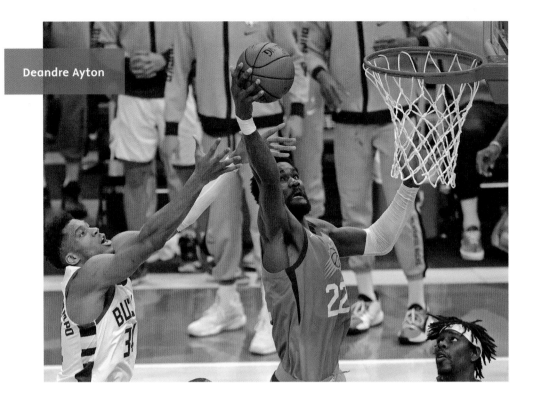

Deandre Ayton

teamed with Paul's 9 assists and 16 points a game as the Suns recorded 51 wins. They returned to the playoffs for the first time in 11 years. They easily won the first three rounds. They met the Milwaukee Bucks in the NBA Finals. Booker and Paul combined for 113 points as Phoenix won the first two games. Milwaukee took the next four to claim the championship.

The Suns started the 2021–22 season by losing three of their first four games. Then they roared to 18 wins in a row and finished with a franchise- and league-best 64 wins. Their record was even more impressive because Paul suffered a broken thumb just before the All-Star break. He missed 15 games. Center Deandre Ayton took up some of the slack. He averaged more than 17 points while shooting more than 63 percent from the field. Monty Williams was named NBA Coach of the Year.

But in the playoffs, shadows began to eclipse the Suns. They needed six games—which included Paul's record-setting performance—to defeat the Pelicans. New Orleans had barely squeezed into the playoffs with just 36 wins.

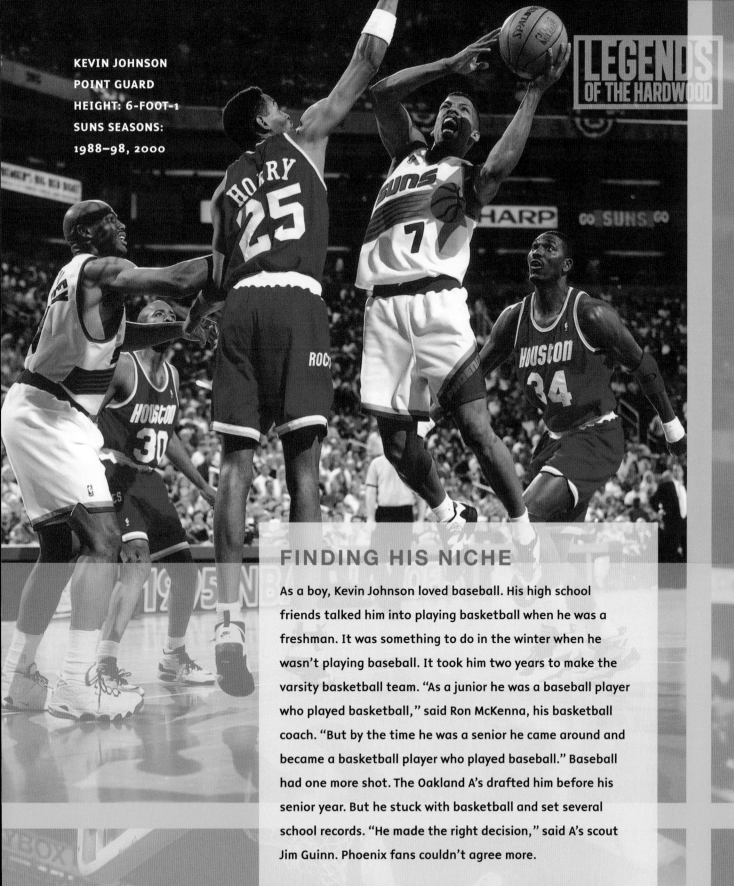

KEVIN JOHNSON
POINT GUARD
HEIGHT: 6-FOOT-1
SUNS SEASONS:
1988–98, 2000

FINDING HIS NICHE

As a boy, Kevin Johnson loved baseball. His high school
friends talked him into playing basketball when he was a
freshman. It was something to do in the winter when he
wasn't playing baseball. It took him two years to make the
varsity basketball team. "As a junior he was a baseball player
who played basketball," said Ron McKenna, his basketball
coach. "But by the time he was a senior he came around and
became a basketball player who played baseball." Baseball
had one more shot. The Oakland A's drafted him before his
senior year. But he stuck with basketball and set several
school records. "He made the right decision," said A's scout
Jim Guinn. Phoenix fans couldn't agree more.

PHOENIX SUNS

Devin Booker

The Suns faced Dallas in the conference semifinals. The Suns won the first two games. The Mavericks took the next two. Phoenix won Game 5. Dallas took a 60–45 halftime lead in Game 6. They cruised to a 113–86 win. That set up a decisive Game 7 in Phoenix. The Suns had won all three home games thus far in the series. Their average winning margin was 19 points.

What followed was one of the most lopsided—and unexpected—wins in NBA playoff history. The Mavericks upset the Suns, 123–90. Phoenix scored just 27 points in the first half. So did a single Dallas player, guard Luka Dončić. The Mavericks had a 30-point lead at that point. They extended their lead to as much as 46 points. The Phoenix collapse extended through the entire team. Paul didn't score a field goal until Dallas led by 40 points. He finished with 10 points. Booker was 3-for-14 from the field. He had 11 points. "We basically played the worst game of the season tonight," said coach Monty Williams. "Couldn't make a shot early, and that messed with us a little bit." It was a thoroughly disappointing end to an otherwise historically successful season.

Pumpkinville was one of several names suggested before Phoenix was selected as the city's name in the 1860s. It didn't take the Suns long to become Cinderella. They turned their pumpkin into an elegant carriage that consistently carried them to the play-offs in their early years. But then the clock seemed to strike midnight. The Suns went back to scrubbing pots while their sister teams were dancing in the playoffs. The most recent seasons have let fans believe their team will soon find another glass slipper and finally capture that elusive first NBA title.

Mikal Bridges

INDEX